Rigorous Grading Using Microsoft Word® AutoCorrect

Plus Google Docs®

ERIK BEAN, ED.D.

WESTPHALIA PRESS
An imprint of Policy Studies Organization

Also from Westphalia Press

westphaliapress.org

The Idea of the Digital University

France and New England
Volumes 1, 2, & 3

Treasures of London

The History of Photography

L'Enfant and the Freemasons

Baronial Bedrooms

Making Trouble for Muslims

Material History and
Ritual Objects

Paddle Your Own Canoe

Opportunity and Horatio Alger

Careers in the Face of Challenge

Bookplates of the Kings

Collecting American Presidential
Autographs

Freemasonry in Old Buffalo

Young Freemasons?

Social Satire and the
Modern Novel

The Essence of Harvard

Ivanhoe Masonic Quartettes

A Definitive Commentary
on Bookplates

James Martineau and
Rebuilding Theology

No Bird Lacks Feathers

Gilded Play

Earthworms, Horses, and
Living Things

The Man Who Killed
President Garfield

Anti-Masonry and the
Murder of Morgan

Understanding Art

Homeopathy

Fishing the Florida Keys

Collecting Old Books

Masonic Secret Signs and
Passwords

The Thomas Starr King Dispute

Earl Warren's Masonic Lodge

Lariats and Lassos

Mr. Garfield of Ohio

The Wisdom of Thomas
Starr King

The French Foreign Legion

War in Syria

Naturism Comes to the
United States

New Sources on Women and
Freemasonry

Designing, Adapting, Strategizing
in Online Education

Gunboat and Gun-runner

Meeting Minutes of Naval Lodge
No. 4 F.A.A.M

Rigorous Grading Using Microsoft Word® AutoCorrect

Plus Google Docs®

Westphalia Press
An imprint of Policy Studies Organization
1527 New Hampshire Ave., NW
Washington, D.C. 20036
info@ipsonet.org

ISBN-13: 978-1-63391-074-4
ISBN-10: 1633910741

Cover and Interior design by Taillefer Long at Illuminated Stories:
www.illuminatedstories.com

Daniel Gutierrez-Sandoval, Executive Director
PSO and Westphalia Press

Devin Proctor, Director of Media and Publications
PSO and Westphalia Press

Updated material and comments on this edition
can be found at the Westphalia Press website:
www.westphaliapress.org

TABLE OF CONTENTS

INTRODUCTION   1

AFFIXING AUTOCORRECT TO QUICK ACCESS TOOLBAR   3

FIVE STEPS TO ENABLE AUTO COMMENTING   5

TIME SAVING IDEAS FOR DOWNLOADING, NAMING...
..STUDENT PAPERS, AND ELECTRONIC GRADEBOOK ENTRY   7

APPENDIX A: APA & GRAMMAR DETAILED...
...FEEDBACK SAMPLES   11

APPENDIX B: ABSORBING AND DISPENSING PICTURES   25

APPENDIX C: SOUND AND VIDEO COMMENTS   27

APPENDIX D: MLA FEEDBACK QUICK TIPS   29

APPENDIX E: ENABLE AUTOCORRECT...
...PRIOR TO WORD 2007   33

APPENDIX F: ENABLE AUTOCORRECT...
...IN WORD FOR MAC LINK   35

APPENDIX G: AUTOCORRECT BACKUP UTILITY TIPS   37

APPENDIX H: ENABLE AUTOCORRECT ACTION.......
.......IN GOOGLE DOCS   39

REFERENCES   41

ABOUT THE AUTHOR   43

INTRODUCTION

It was an exciting time for me during June 2009. I was on my way to Honolulu, Hawaii as a University of Phoenix faculty member and College of Arts and Sciences chair, Detroit campus, to present a paper at the World Conference on Educational Multimedia, Hypermedia and Telecommunications, similarly titled to this booklet (Bean, 2009). As a busy chair and faculty member I searched for methods to grade student papers faster, but with as much rigor as any written feedback any department chair would expect.

The answer was always right in front of me. The answer was Microsoft Word AutoCorrect, a feature that has been on every edition of Word more than 20 years. AutoCorrect had always been standing by to automatically correct simple typing errors such as occasional misspelled words, but I wanted to see how far I could stretch those corrections. I quickly discovered by just setting up simple shortcut acronyms and pressing the spacebar I could insert whole paragraphs of text, rubrics, tables—colorized, in bold, underlined—and a grading revolution of canned feedback was underway!

Soothsayers could have predicted some traditional faculty members would cry foul due to the assembly line nature of these comments, but of course in between these canned comments; one should customize feedback for each student including a summary of positive and rigorous — formative and summative feedback.

If you want the most thorough grading experience that includes having Word tell you the grade level of the student's writing and percentage of passive voice enable these important metrics inside the grammar settings. To do so follow this link: http://tinyurl.com/k3n8fev to my step-by-step article aboard my Examiner.com blog (Bean, 2010). Soon you'll be prepared to grade at lightning bolt speed! That's probably why the folks at Microsoft used a lightning bolt to denote the AutoCorrect icon.

AFFIXING AUTOCORRECT
TO QUICK ACCESS TOOLBAR

Using Microsoft Word AutoCorrect to grade papers can save much time compared to grading hardcopy assignments. Many schools are only accepting formal papers in an electronic format for documentation and archive purposes. The substantive feedback comment suggestions here are geared for grades 9–12 and higher education papers. Please note the electronic comments suggested in Appendix A: APA & Grammar Detailed Feedback Samples can be modified for your particular needs.

The comments presented do not include traditional English symbols but you can insert these via instructions in Appendix B: Absorbing and Dispensing Pictures. Other helpful information is located in the following appendices: Appendix C: Sound and Video Comments, See Appendix D: MLA Feedback Quick Tips, Appendix E: Enable AutoCorrect Prior to Word 2007, Appendix F: Enable AutoCorrect in Word for MAC, Appendix G: AutoCorrect Backup Utility, and finally Appendix H: Enabling AutoCorrect Action in Google Docs.

Five preliminary steps will help you to quickly access AutoCorrect every time you want to add a new comment that may be dispensed at the keyboard. To prepare Word 2007 through 2013 to instantly insert pre-written comments about APA style, grammar, thesis development, or any text that would benefit the student, the process starts with the top menu bar known as the *Quick Access Toolbar*.

1. First, at the top Word menu bar locate the drop down icon as shown here. Click this icon to expand the menu.

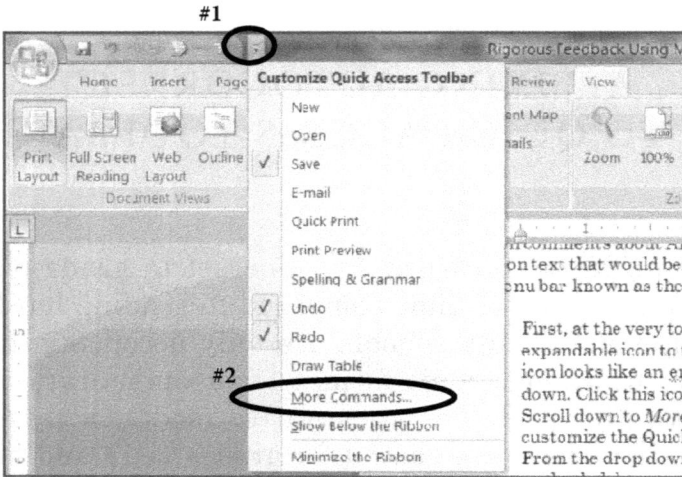

2. Scroll down to *More Commands* and select. This will allow you to customize the Quick Access Toolbar.

3. From the drop down menu in the upper left change the preloaded drop menu options from *Popular Commands* to *All Commands*.

4. Scroll down to *AutoCorrect Options* and highlight.

5. Click *Add* to send this time saving feature to your Quick Access Tool Bar list. Finally, click *OK* (not shown) to permanently affix.

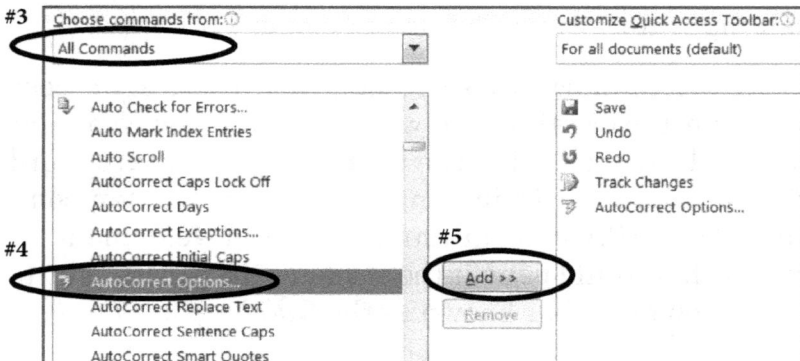

FIVE STEPS TO ENABLE
AUTO COMMENTING

Now, in just five steps, you will be ready to start grading rigorously and faster than ever before. The Auto-Correct icon looks like a bar with a bolt of lightning. If you see this on your top menu, you are now ready to load your word template with a host of never-ending feedback comments, rubrics, and pictures, audio, and video if you wish.

1. Begin to compile your frequently used feedback comments by opening up a new document and make certain the tracking feature is off. You can construct these comments off the top of your head or copy and paste them from the appendices. The process to absorb the comments will be done one comment at a time.

2. After you have typed and formatted your first comment (use of lower case in most instances is suggested, but one may want to bold or use an attention getting color), highlight the comment with your mouse.

3. Now click the *AutoCorrect* yellow lightning bolt icon in the Quick Access menu bar. This will automatically insert the text into your normal.doc template file.

4. However, before clicking *OK*, you must assign an acronym or other single word or code that you will type and follow with a single space bar click. Do select *Formatted text* if you are including color or

style changes. In addition, you will not be limited to the 256 characters that plain text only allows. Click *OK* to save your new AutoCorrect comment.

5. Write down the acronym so you will have an immediate record of all the ones you created. In Appendix G we will show you how to back up and reinstate all of your acronyms and comments should you obtain a new version of Word or simply want to port these to another computer. You can then have a complete record of your acronyms and comments.

In addition to developing your own acronym structure, common words with an extra letter at the end can help you to remember and will not set off the AutoCorrect insert when composing other word processing documents since the extra letter makes that word unusual.

For example, instead of applying an acronym one might want to use the word *header*. Remember, every time that word is typed and the space bar is pressed, the AutoCorrect comment stored will be inserted. However, by adding an extra letter *r* (headerr), for example, at the end of this word, AutoCorrect will only then be set off. By applying extra letters or other symbols, you can avoid setting off unwanted AutoCorrect comments, but still have a word that is easy to remember.

Finally, if you've inserted an acronym, pressed the space bar, and the word is not inserted, it could mean you began the acronym right next to another word. Be sure to allow at least one space before you start typing an acronym that was preloaded in AutoCorrect.

TIME SAVING IDEAS FOR DOWNLOADING, NAMING STUDENT PAPERS, AND ELECTRONIC GRADEBOOK ENTRY

If your online platform requires you to download student papers to a folder or directory on your hard drive, it is suggested that students be required to use a file naming convention with a minimum of their first name and last initial. Using a naming convention will save the instructor grading time. Suggested syllabus language to require students to use such a file name could read like this:

All assignments must be uploaded and submitted to your Individual Assignment box/folder/account. All assignments that require a Word.doc attachment should be named using your first name, last initial, followed by an underscore, and the main assignment name (or week it is due).

For example:

MaryD_Wk1.doc.

There are several benefits of requiring the student to use his or her first name as well as an extended file name. However, these benefits will not likely work if your online platform allows you to download all the files at once. If this is the case, each paper will be contained inside each student's folder.

1. The instructor can easily reference the student by first name during the grading process just by looking up at the top of the open window to view the student's name. Personalizing the paper with the student's name provides a sense of immediacy creating a positive relationship between student and instructor (Mehrabian, 2007). No longer is it necessary to scroll up to the cover page to remember the student's name.

2. The instructor can more easily download and better categorize such assignment files by week, by team, by topic based on the required category following the underscore.

3. Finally, to save more time during grading, once these individual student files are downloaded, the instructor can (a) highlight all the files collectively by clicking on the first file to highlight it, (b) scroll down to the last file in the list, and (c) while holding down the shift key, right click and select "Open" so all files open simultaneously. These steps only work on a PC.

4. After using AutoCorrect to grade, rename the file, with the score of the paper earned in the file name itself. For example, MaryD_Wk1_89.doc. When it is time to manually enter grades into an electronic type grade book system, the instructor can simply open the directory or folder where the assignments are stored, view the individual score coupled with the student name as shown in the file name itself.

When it comes to substantive student paper feedback, particularly repetitive feedback comments, Word AutoCorrect is a great choice. By supplementing these canned comments with personalized remarks representing your unique subject matter expertise, grading can be done faster and more consistently between students. Consistency in grading can set a new department standard in your school's core curriculum and no longer may students complain they did not receive consistent substantive feedback.

APPENDIX A:
APA & GRAMMAR DETAILED
FEEDBACK SAMPLES

The suggested shortcut acronym or word appears above each canned feedback comment sample. Remember, AutoCorrect can only absorb one acronym and comment at a time.

1. Take a comment from the list below and copy it to an open Microsoft Word page.

2. Then highlight the sample.

3. Click the AutoCorrect icon in the Quick Access Toolbar and it will absorb the comment.

4. Input an acronym of your choice.

5. After you check either save as Text or Formatted in the radio dial box, then select *OK*, Word will permanently assign the acronym and dispense the feedback comment each time you type it and hit the space bar.

To follow are examples that align to the American Psychological Association Style Manual, Ver. 6 (American Psychological Association, 2009). Remember, you can always modify these samples before highlighting them with your cursor and absorbing them one at a time into AutoCorrect. In addition, you can come up with your own acronyms, ones that you can remember based on your own system. Add colored text, bolding, or shading to these comments as you deem appropriate.

aFont < Enter this acronym or one you like better after you highlight the comment below and click the AutoCorrect lightning bolt icon. Then click OK to save. Repeat for any canned comment or acronym you like below:

Font not APA style. Only Times New Roman is acceptable and in 12-point size double spaced according to APA 6th Ed.

Allr

All references must appear matched based on author last name or title in the paper body. Or, your material is considered plagiarized since you did not denote in text attribution for your paraphrasing and/or quotes.

Alwayss

Always submit cover letter/check list/questionnaire and essay as one file attachment.:)

Bt

Better language here! Much more professional, non-bias, and more prominent third-person voice!

Conc

Do not say in conclusion. Summarize major thesis variable defenses discussed in the body. The reader knows you are concluding because in addition to the major defenses, the writer must restate the thesis.

Cont

Contractions are not allowed in college essays/ research papers. Spell out words completely.

Dbl

Double spacing required throughout the entire paper including the reference page.

Gd

< Nice detail here that is helpful to the reader and your topic in general.

Gd1

Good critical thinking on the topic in general.

Gd2

Very good writing voice supported by examples. In all subsequent essays, be sure to switch to a third-person writing voice and use properly documented in-text APA/MLA style paraphrasing and quotes to support thesis defense.

Gd3

Very good authoritative writing voice that sounds bias free, inviting, and succinct.

Gdw

< good word choice that adds value and clarity to your critical thinking for the reader.

DQ

Direct quote in MLA/APA style is needed to support your suppositions and defend your thesis.

Continued...

Ethos1

ethos is the qualifications of the writer. Discuss how the writer's personal experience is used in the published piece.

Gd

< Nice detail here that is helpful to the reader and your topic in general.

Gd1

Good critical thinking on the topic in general.

Gd2

Very good writing voice supported by examples. In all subsequent essays, be sure to switch to a third-person writing voice and use properly documented in-text APA/MLA style paraphrasing and quotes to support thesis defense.

Gdw

< good word choice that adds value and clarity to your critical thinking for the reader.

Gr

< Grammar issue. Wording or punctuation.

Hist

Typically, the first paragraph in the body is the historical perspective. (1) How did the situation get started? (2) How did it change over time? (3) Where does the situation stand today? These are written in statements, not questions of course. Encapsulate. Provide definitions of the key terms first. Do this first before defending a valid thesis.

Incomp

< Incomplete sentence. Either adjoin to previous sentence or following sentence.

ind

Indent must be .5 inches new school or ½ inch old school.

Ital

Italicize special words in APA/MLA. Do not use quotes unless followed by a citation.

Leng

You have exceeded the length. Please check the assignment requirements.

Ld0

The lead sentences should be about the topic in general, not a stance. :)

Ld2

Excellent, creative, lead paper statements that make the reader want more! Nice work here :)

Misse1

Ethos may be present if the personal qualifications of the writer comes into the published works. While we know he wrote it, we need to make a more finer distinction of his/her background and what specific text is related to it.

Continued...

Misslit

Missing focus on ethos, pathos, or logos. You must demonstrate you know the definitions and where in the text these might be used. Pathos is emotion. Name the emotion, show the text, for example.

Misslite

< thus ethos is exemplified as the author was active in history during this time period and worked that knowledge into her creative works.

Mostl

< most literary work contains all three rhetorical styles of ethos, pathos, and logos. Focus on the most prominent and place thesis always as the last sentence in the introduction :)

Mostt

Most authors use all three: ethos, pathos, and logos. You must focus on the most prominent one or two only.

Neverr

Never say what the paper will do. Instead make definitive required introductory statements.

Pathos1

Name the emotions and immediately include a direct quote to defend your stance. :)

Continued...

Perio

Period always goes outside last parenthesis in an MLA/APA citation, unless a block quote is used. In that case, the period goes at the sentence end. Also, if a block quote is used, no formal quotation marks are added.

Pla

PLAGIARIZED! YOU MUST INCLUDE DIRECT QUOTES REGARD-LESS OF LISTING AN AUTHOR. YOU TOOK THESE WORDS VERBATIM! CHANGE INTO YOUR OWN WORDS IF NOT QUOTING

Pleasee

Please do not use first-person overtones. They appear bias. Instead, substitute the word for the subject. For example, Americans, people, society, or one.

Pg

Page number OR paragraph number (Website only) from where the quote was found must accompany all MLA/APA style direct quote in-text citations. For MLA paraphrasing, do not include page number if author name is cited.

Rcon

You did not meet the objective satisfactorily. You must include signal phrases that introduce direct quotes and/or paraphrases to better support honed thesis suppositions.

Continued...

Rcon1

You met the objective satisfactorily, but need to provide more substantive signal phrases that introduce direct quotes and/or paraphrases to better support your suppositions.

Rcon2

Good use of research featuring signal phrases that introduce germane paraphrases and quotes.

Rcon3

Excellent defense supported by well-researched paraphrasing and/or quoting. You should be proud of this effort!

Rcon4

Good topic and good attribution. Missing link to a valid honed thesis, however.

Runn

RUNNING HEAD MISSING, Or WORDS MISSING: YOU MUST PHYSICALLY LIST THE WORDS – Running head – in lower case. OR! Words (TITLE) AFTER RUNNING HEAD MUST BE IN ALL CAPS. Check that Running head is now located inside header according to APA Manual 6th Ed. Page number is required in the upper right-hand corner of header. Running head is left justified. Running head is not located by page number.

Starend

Citations should only appear at sentence start according to Adams (2010) or sentence end (Adams, 2010). Period always goes outside the last parenthesis.

Subj

Subject verb singular agreement needed.

Threee

Three or more authors, the writer must revert to using only the primary author followed by et al. when citation is at the end of a sentence. However, if you chose to introduce the sentence referencing the authors at the start, all three or more must be listed and the last one is separated by and. Other rules apply. Check APA Manual for details.

Tips

A thesis is a contract to the reader regarding what the paper is about. A thesis is not based on your opinion, although you may agree with it. Every key word you choose must be documented in the paper, supported via quotes, and paraphrasing from published sources. Remember, you must write in a third-person voice. The thesis is always the last sentence in the introductory paragraph. A thesis should not be trite, it should be more controversial, contemporary, and must be supported in the body of the paper. The thesis must be written in the student author's own third person voice. Good news! A thesis can only be one sentence long. In addition to two or three variables based on key nomenclature (terminology) in the discipline chosen, one must tie a thesis to something meaningful to avoid editorializing. Editorialized example: Michigan should repeal its mandatory motorcycle helmet law. Valid thesis example: If Michigan repeals its mandatory motorcycle helmet law, it may earn more than $3 million in revenue from lodging, restaurants, and medical attention. < Three variables at the end tied something meaningful revenue.

Tips2

The thesis must be all encompassing to the reader. In other words, one must be able to read it and know exactly what the stance is as well as the topic regardless of the introductory sentences preceding it.

Tipseval

List the specific make, brand, model number, and benefits and/or drawbacks for review in the thesis here!

Tipslit

< This is not a literary analysis thesis. Which rhetorical strategies were most prominent in the piece? Ethos, pathos, or logos, for example, and what was the overall lesson are aims of the essay?

Tipslit1

Instead of saying what the essay will do, in the thesis, develop a firm rhetorical based stance. Authors Hawthorne, Beecher Stowe, Poe, and Thoreau used intriguing forms of pathos to do X, Y, and Z < always tie a thesis to something meaningful, the historical context of the day. I hope that helps. :)

Twoo

Cannot quote two different sources in same paragraph. You may paraphrase one and quote the other.

Sirr

Sir names are not used in academic writing. Reduce everyone to their last name whenever possible.

Continued...

Youu

You have gone too long without an MLA/APA in-text paraphrase citation or quote We do not defend a thesis based on our personal experience. One must always cite published research or commentary to defend such a thesis.

Yr

Year in parenthesis must follow all authors like (2011). < period must be included as well.

Vol

In APA one should never spell out volume or abbreviate, nor should one spell out issue or abbreviate it. You should identify volume, issue, and page numbers in APA when they are available through the article or database. Here is a sample 24(10), 12-15. The first number is italicized; it is the volume number. The second number with no spaces between the volume and first parenthesis is the issue number surrounded by parentheses. The issue number is not italicized. The last numbers preceded by a comma are the page numbers. These are not italicized and should account for the start page and end page numbers followed by a period.

Youuv

You have gone too long without defending a valid thesis variable.

Continued...

Rubric1 < Before inserting this acronym in Auto-Correct, be certain to highlight the entire rubric below from Mechanics through the Total. AutoCorrect will absorb it all! Tips for other rubrics: Also consider creating an A, A?, B+, B, B?, C+, C, C?, D+, D, D?, F pre-scored rubric based on the most common grade range errors typically observed and then modify the points along with personalized comments. Either way, you'll save much time compared to copying and pasting as well as adding up rubrics from scratch. Finally, note that auto correct will absorb tables if you prefer your rubrics that way.

Mechanics, 10/

Mechanics refers to the overall theme/agreement of the paper as it relates to the introductory statements and/or a properly developed thesis.

Grammar/Punctuation/Spelling, 30/

Grammar refers to proper sentence construction, avoidance of run-ons, awkward, or incomplete thoughts. Issues surrounding tenses or pluralism, for example. Proper and consistent use of adverbs to precede or proceed a source.

Punctuation refers to location of quotes, use of ellipsis, proper use of apostrophes, commas, em-dashes, n-dashes, colons, and semi-colons. Avoidance of dangling modifiers and contractions, misuse of direct quotes regardless of other APA style issues satisfied.

Spelling refers to the words spelled correctly or are the wrong words used and misspelled.

Continued...

Content/Development of ideas/Organization, 30/

Content refers to the depth and appropriateness of research (secondary) attribution paid inside the body of the paper. Content also refers to the academic writing voice.

Development of Ideas refers to how earlier topics, not necessarily thesis related, introduced in the paper are discussed, followed up, and concluded

Organization refers to proper use and development of the introduction, historical, statement/thesis, body, and conclusion.

Formatting/Sentence Variety/Style/Creativity, 30/

Sentence Variety refers to paragraph development, clarity, and completeness. In addition, it includes the use of long and short sentences, the use of chronology, conjunctions, coordinates, and occasional semi-colons to add variety.

Style denotes whether the paper has been put in the proper APA style or any other style requirements the facilitator has requested.

Creativity refers to the breadth and depth of analogies, overall theme development, and intrigue the author has presented.

Total: 100 _____

APPENDIX B:
ABSORBING AND
DISPENSING PICTURES

While one can always click insert and select any image to include in any Word document, you may find it beneficial to create a series of more complicated or detail images, such as a special flowchart that denotes writing processes, mathematical detailed steps, or pictures of traditional grammar symbols. No matter the use, typing an acronym at the keyboard to dispense the picture is much faster than clicking insert and locating the file.

The process for absorbing and dispensing pictures via AutoCorrect is similar to highlighting, absorbing, and assigning an acronym for text.

1. Reexamine *Five Steps for Enabling Auto Commenting* if needed.

2. Instead of writing out a comment while a Word document is open, have an available photo or other image you created and via the Insert menu tab, and clicking Picture place the image either on a current paper you are grading or just a blank page to begin absorbing any number of pictures, one at a time of course.

3. Highlight the picture with your cursor and click the AutoCorrect lightning bolt icon located in the Quick Access Toolbar.

4. Apply an acronym of your choice then click the radio dial box labeled formatted then click *OK* to save.

5. Repeat Steps 1–4 for all the images you wish to be available in AutoCorrect.

6. Finally, every time you type the acronym and press the space bar, the picture will be dispensed!

7. Be sure to save a list of your acronyms if you are not going to immediately back them up via the available utility and instructions in Appendix G.

APPENDIX C:
SOUND AND VIDEO COMMENTS

Imagine your student examining the feedback you provided in his or her essay. He starts reading and instead of just seeing an inserted comment, he sees the symbol for a WMA recording, one that is labeled like this:

TipsForHistoricalPerspective.wma

This recording was me reminding a student named John on what a Historical Perspective paragraph contains and where it should be located in a typical essay. You will need to create your recording first using the PC accessory dubbed Sound Recorder, save the file to a directory on your PC, and then under the *Insert* menu tab select *Object* located in the upper right menu. Then choose *Create from File*. Now the audio file will be dispensed in your open Word document. To absorb the audio file into AutoCorrect repeat similar steps 2 through 5 shown under **Five Steps to Enable Auto Commenting.**

Bear in mind that dispensing an audio or video comment as you grade will increase the file size adding to upload and download times.

Other audio recording considerations:

1. Maintain an authoritative yet friendly voice.

2. Like any good recording, be certain there are no other annoying or extraneous background sounds.

3. Most PCs have built in microphones so it is not necessary to purchase or use a separate one.

4. When saving the file name know that the entire name will be viewable to the student. Therefore, carefully select a name that reflects the type of feedback to be dispensed.

5. For MAC students be sure to save the recording as an MP3 and the video as an MPG4 for compatibility. Insert via the Object menu item. Follow the instructions as designated above.

APPENDIX D:
MLA FEEDBACK QUICK TIPS

The suggested shortcut acronym or word appears above each canned feedback comment sample. Remember, Auto-Correct can only absorb one acronym and comment at a time.

1. Take a comment from the list below and copy it to an open Microsoft Word page.

2. Then highlight the sample.

3. Click the AutoCorrect icon in the Quick Access Toolbar and it will absorb the comment.

4. Input an acronym of your choice.

5. After you check either save as Text or Formatted in the radio dial box, then select *OK*, Word will permanently assign the acronym and dispense the feedback comment each time you type it and hit the space bar.

To follow are examples that align to the MLA style 6th Ed. (Modern Language Association, 2009). Remember, you can always modify these samples before highlighting them with your cursor and absorbing them one at a time into AutoCorrect. Add colored text, bolding, or shading to these comments as you deem appropriate. Since the APA section earlier contained many grammar and essay construction comments, this section is much shorter. Use the acronyms suggested below or create your own.

mFont < Enter this acronym or one you like better after you highlight the comment below and click the AutoCorrect lightning bolt icon. Then click OK to save. Repeat for any canned comment or acronym you like below.

Font should be Times New Roman or Ariel and in 12 point font.

mTi

Title which should appear after skipping one space from the MLA cover matter, should have a newsworthy creative appeal. No more than 15 words.

mHd

Header is missing or does not include all necessary style information. It should include a page number flush right. Your last name which should appear in upper and lower case based on capitalization of your pronoun has one space between it and the page number.

mCv

Missing required MLA cover information or layout is incorrect. See proper layout below:

14 July 2014

mRft

MLA says the bibliography should be listed only as Works Cited, centered on reference page.

mWC

Proper formatting for MLA reference page has errors. See sample of required information below:

WORKS CITED

Author's last name, first. <u>Title of Book</u>. City:
Publisher, Year.

Author's last name, first. "Title of Article."
Publication Title, Date Published: Pages.

Author's last name, first. "Title of Online
Article." *Online Publication Title,* Version
(Year?): Pages. Date Accessed <Web address>.

"Title of Article." *Title of Media*. CD-ROM,
DVD. City: Publisher, Year.

APPENDIX E:
ENABLE AUTOCORRECT PRIOR TO WORD 2007

To do the same in Word 1997 through 2003:

1. Go to *Tools* and scroll down to *AutoCorrect*.

2. Do this after you highlight canned text you have created in your Word.doc. Please note that in either instance of Word, only one auto comment can be highlighted at a time and assigned shortcut keys.

3. Do carefully categorize your shortcut key words to remind you of what will be automatically inserted.

4. The next time you open and grade a paper, your pre-loaded comments will be standing by awaiting your typed word command.

5. If you should ever not want to insert the comment, simply click the *Undo* icon that should also be loaded to your top menu bar. Then continue writing or grading.

Now you will be ready to grade papers much faster and with less wear and tear on your phalanges!

APPENDIX F:
ENABLE AUTOCORRECT
IN WORD FOR MAC LINK

Microsoft's instructions located at either of the addresses listed below can be used to get to AutoCorrect in your Microsoft Word for MAC program (Microsoft Corporation, 2014). Then follow all other steps in this booklet under *Five Steps to Enable Auto Commenting*. Load with any of the APA, MLA, audio, or picture suggestions located in the appendices and add your own custom comments as you deem necessary.

- http://office.microsoft.com/en-us/mac-word-help/add-or-edit-automatic-corrections-HA102927227.aspx or

- http://tinyurl.com/lqt8hol.

APPENDIX G:
AUTOCORRECT BACKUP
UTILITY TIPS

If you ever change your computer or update to the latest version of Word, please know that you must back up your AutoCorrect comments before doing so. I have had good luck downloading and running an AutoCorrect backup program from MT Herald at the following virus and adware free URL. This was again tested as recently as June 2014.

- http://mtherald.com/free-autocorrect-backup-and-restore-utility-for-microsoft-word/ or

- http://tinyurl.com/l39fy8p.

  The concept is simple.

  1. The program finds the correct Word file that contains all the current AutoCorrect comments you have stored and backs this file up.

  2. You then save this file as any Word document in a directory you know you can remember.

  3. Another file the program contains is a macro disguised as a Word document. It is a good idea to save this file to the same directory.

  4. When you open the file it will immediately provide you three options: Back Up, Restore, or Cancel.

5.   If you choose Back Up it will find the latest Auto-Correct file and again provide it to you.

6.   If you choose restore, it will ask you to select the file you wish to restore from, the last AutoCorrect file you backed up.

Microsoft offers its own steps to doing this but is more time consuming:

- http://office.microsoft.com/en-us/word-help/move-autocorrect-entries-between-computers-in-word-HA001034913.aspx or

- http://tinyurl.com/khx9baf.

APPENDIX H:
ENABLE AUTOCORRECT
ACTION IN GOOGLE DOCS

Many K-12 schools and people are flocking to Google Docs. No worries. Google Docs allows for a similar insert comment action but only in text form and it requires an extra copy and paste step. To begin, start:

1. With your Google Doc open, click the Tools menu located midway at the top navigational menu bar.

2. Scroll down to preferences and select.

3. At the top of the new window you will notice two boxes: *Replace* and *With*.

4. The Replace text is the acronym you type at the keyboard to create the AutoCorrect action.

5. The *With* text could be any number of APA, MLA, or any other style comments you wish to add.

6. Type in your *Replace* acronym.

7. Copy and paste the *With* comment as you have constructed it in an open Google Doc or one you copy and paste from the suggestions in previous appendices here.

8. Click *OK* to save.

Note that more comments can be added by scrolling up the Preferences window via the right-hand scroll bar before clicking OK to save. Repeat steps 1–8 above to add more comments.

Good News! There is no need to ever back up your Google Docs AutoCorrect comments since they are stored on Google's server regardless of the computer you access. The current drawback is that since the comments are in text they are more difficult for the student to discern unless you go back and highlight them, or perhaps insert a space above and below each comment. Finally, be aware that unless you write down the acronym to remember it, you can only peruse through the window to see what you've stored.

REFERENCES

American Psychological Association. (2009). *Publication Manual of the American Psychological Association,* Sixth Edition. Washington, DC: American Psychological Association.

Bean, E. (2009). "Step-by-step Instructions for Rigorous Feedback Using Microsoft Word Autocorrect," in *Proceedings of World Conference on Educational Multimedia, Hypermedia and Telecommunications 2009.* Chesapeake, VA: AACE, pp. 2090-2094.

Bean, E. (2010). "Write Right, Re-enable Word Spell Checker." http://www.examiner.com/article/write-right-re enable-word-spell-checker

Mehrabian, A. (2007). Nonverbal Communications, New Brunswick, NJ: Aldine Transaction.

Microsoft Corporation. (2014). "Add or Edit Automatic Corrections." http://office.microsoft.com/en-us/mac-word-help/add-or-edit-automatic-corrections-HA102927227.aspx

Modern Language Association. (2009). *MLA Handbook for Writers of Research Papers.* New York: Modern Language Association.

ABOUT THE AUTHOR

Erik Bean, Ed.D. is currently an associate professor of arts and humanities at American Public University. He has served as a department chair, dean, curriculum developer, online instructor, and has taught English composition, mass media, film, and writing for the professions for more than 15 years. He is a motivational speaker and author of a popular book series featuring the use of social media for writing lessons. His conference presentations help teachers do their job efficiently. See other books by Erik Bean including:

Word Press for Student Writing Projects: Aligned to Common Core Standards by Erik Bean and Emily Waszak (Feb 25, 2014)
Published by Brigantine Media/Compass Books, St. Johnsbury, VT.
Print and Kindle Edition.
For more information visit: SocialMediaLessonPlans.com

Argumentative Essay Instructional Curriculum: Incorporating Companion English Language Arts Standards Simultaneously by Teacher 1Stop.com and Erik Bean (Oct 1, 2013)
Published by Deadline Communications[sm]
Kindle Edition.

Informational Text Essay Instructional Curriculum II: Incorporating Companion English Language Arts Standards by Teacher 1Stop and Erik Bean (Apr 22, 2014)
Published by Deadline Communications[sm]
Kindle Edition.

Visit Erik Bean's Amazon.com author page for all available books: http://tinyurl.com/mbopdoj

www.ingramcontent.com/pod-product-compliance
Lightning Source LLC
Chambersburg PA
CBHW060042050426
42448CB00012B/3109